Contents

Some words are shown in bold, **like this**. You can find them in the glossary on page 23.

What are jars and pots?

A jar is a round **container** with a lid.

Most jars are made of glass.

o Riches

d Pots

Daniel Nunn

www.raintreepublishers.co.uk
Visit our website to find out more information about Raintree books.

To order:
☎ Phone 0845 6044371
🖹 Fax +44 (0) 1865 312263
🖳 Email myorders@raintreepublishers.co.uk

Customers from outside the UK please telephone +44 1865 312262

Raintree is an imprint of Capstone Global Library Limited, a company incorporated in England and Wales having its registered office at 7 Pilgrim Street, London, EC4V 6LB – Registered company number: 6695582

Edited by Rebecca Rissman, Daniel Nunn, and Sian Smith
Designed by Joanna Hinton-Malivoire
Picture research by Tracy Cummins
Originated by Capstone Global Library Ltd
Printed and bound in China by South China Printing Company Ltd

ISBN 978 1 406 22681 2 (hardback)
15 14 13 12 11
10 9 8 7 6 5 4 3 2 1

ISBN 978 1 406 22688 1 (paperback)
16 15 14 13 12
10 9 8 7 6 5 4 3 2 1

British Library Cataloguing in Publication Data
Nunn, Daniel. Jars and pots. – (From rubbish to riches) 1. Handicraft–Juvenile literature.
2. Containers–Recycling 3. Trash art 4. Refuse and refuse disposal 5. Salvage
745.5-dc22
A full catalogue record for this book is available from the British Library.

Acknowledgements
We would like to thank the following for permission to reproduce photographs: Corbis pp. 9, 23d (© Franz-Peter Tschauner/dpa); Heinemann Raintree pp. 6, 8, 10, 11, 12, 13, 14, 15, 16, 17, 18, 19, 20, 21, 23a, 23f (Karon Dubke), 22c (David Rigg); istockphoto pp. 7 (© Serhiy Zavalnyuk), 23e (© Ian Poole); Shutterstock pp. 4 (© donatas1205), 5, 23b (© Robert Gebbie Photography), 22a (© Andy Piatt), 22b (© grynold), 23c (© donatas1205).

Cover photograph of jars, a pot, and jar animals, and back cover photographs of a bird bath and a wind chime reproduced with permission of Heinemann Raintree (Karon Dubke).

Every effort has been made to contact copyright holders of material reproduced in this book. Any omissions will be rectified in subsequent printings if notice is given to the publisher.

A pot is a deep container used for storing things, cooking, or for growing plants.

Many pots are made of **ceramic**.

What happens when you throw jars and pots away?

Jars and pots are very useful.

But when you have finished with them, do you throw them away?

If so, then your jars and pots will end up at a rubbish tip.

They will be buried in the ground and may stay there for a very long time.

What is recycling?

It is much better to **recycle** glass jars than throw them away.

Separate glass jars from your other rubbish and put them in a recycling bin.

The glass things will be collected and taken to a **factory**.

Then the glass will be made into something new.

How can I reuse old jars and pots?

You can also use old jars and pots to make your own new things.

When you have finished with a jar or pot, put it somewhere safe instead of throwing it away.

Soon you will have lots of jars and pots waiting to be reused.

You are ready to turn your rubbish into riches!

What can I make with ceramic pots?

You can use **ceramic** pots to make a bird bath.

Then birds can use it to wash in and drink water.

You can also use flower pots to make a wind chime.

Hang it anywhere and wait for the wind to blow!

What can I make with glass jars?

Old glass jars can be made into beautiful snow globes.

Remember to keep the lids, or the water will fall out!

You can also use an old jam jar to make an **air freshener**.

This jar has **pot-pourri** inside to make a room smell nice.

Have you ever seen a toy fish tank in a jar?

It would make a great father's day present!

You can also use jars and pots to make your own toys.

These baby animals have been made out of baby food jars and a flower pot.

Make your own bits and bobs tree

If your bedroom is always untidy, maybe you should make a bits and bobs tree.

You will need a flower pot, modelling clay, cotton wool, twigs, and some silver paint.

First, roll a large piece of modelling clay and place it in the flower pot.

Then fill the pot with cotton wool, so the modelling clay is hidden.

Next, paint your twigs silver.

You could put them on old newspaper
to keep the table clean.

When the paint has dried, push the twigs
through the cotton wool and into the
modelling clay.

Now you can hang your bits and bobs
on the branches!

Recycling quiz

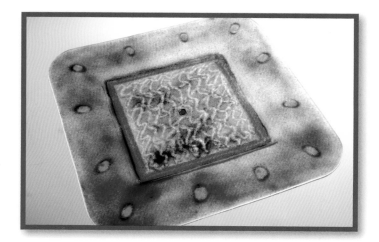

One of these things is made from **recycled** glass. Can you guess which one? (Answer on page 24.)

Glossary

 **air freshener** something that is used to make a room smell nicer

 **ceramic** clay that has been baked in a very hot oven until it is hard

 **container** object used to put things in

 **factory** building where something is made

 **pot-pourri** mixture of dry flowers and spices that smell nice

 **recycle** break down a material and use it again to make something new

Find out more

Ask an adult to help you make fun things with jars and pots using the websites below.

Bird bath: **www.craftsforkids.com/projects/bird_bath.htm**

Snow globe: **http://pbskids.org/zoom/activities/do/snowglobe.html**

Other ideas can be found at the following website. Click on "jars": **http://www.artistshelpingchildren.org/craftsbyitems.html**

Answer to question on page 22
The mat is made from recycled glass.

Index